IDEAS IN PSYCHOANALYSIS

Perversion

Claire Pajaczkowska

Series editor: Ivan Ward

ICON BOOKS UK

TOTEM BOOKS USA

Published in the UK in 2000
by Icon Books Ltd., Grange Road,
Duxford, Cambridge CB2 4QF
email: info@iconbooks.co.uk
www.iconbooks.co.uk

Published in the USA in 2001
by Totem Books
Inquiries to: Icon Books Ltd.,
Grange Road, Duxford,
Cambridge CB2 4QF, UK

Distributed in the UK, Europe,
Canada, South Africa and Asia
by the Penguin Group:
Penguin Books Ltd.,
27 Wrights Lane,
London W8 5TZ

In the United States,
distributed to the trade by
National Book Network Inc.,
4720 Boston Way, Lanham,
Maryland 20706

Published in Australia in 2000
by Allen & Unwin Pty. Ltd.,
PO Box 8500, 9 Atchison Street,
St. Leonards, NSW 2065

Library of Congress catalog
card number applied for

Text copyright © 2000 Claire Pajaczkowska

The author has asserted her moral rights.

Series editor: Ivan Ward

ISBN 1 84046 188 8

Typesetting by Hands Fotoset

Printed and bound in the UK by
Cox & Wyman Ltd., Reading

Perversion

The connotations of the word are unpleasant and have a flavour of morality and therefore of free will that is antiquated in these days of science and determinism.[1]

Thus begins the introduction to the book *Perversion: the Erotic Form of Hatred* – one of the most illuminating and humane explorations of the concept of perversion. And so, if the word has such troubling and antiquated connotations, why is it still in use? Is perversion a sexual act? Is perversion an aggressive act? Do all sexual acts invoke a moral response? Are all aggressive acts unpleasant? What determines the particular fusion of sexuality and aggression that characterises perversion?

The psychoanalytic concept of perversion understands it as a sexual act, but not necessarily a genital act. Even if genitals are used, as in exhibitionism for instance, the genital is not present in its function as adult sexual organ. To understand the paradoxical nature of sex in perversion we need to explore the development of human sexuality, and how infancy and adulthood are connected in that development. There are also perverse acts, such as burglary or addiction, in which no erotic pleasure is consciously experienced, and yet these acts are understood as having a sexual meaning for the subject. How can one concept describe the intense, compelling erotic pleasures of sexuality and also be used to describe acts of criminality, violence and murder? How can one concept account for the pleasures of ordinary sexuality (if any sexuality can be experienced as anything other than extraordinary) and some of the most strange, bizarre and extreme acts of destructiveness, degradation and torture? How is perversion related to concepts of neurosis and psychosis, and also to the experiences of everyday life?

There is considerable controversy over the definition of perversion. Some say it is a matter of variant forms of human sexuality; others think of it as an 'aberrant' form (see Key Terms on page 76). It is only in psychoanalysis that the concept has a diagnostic and descriptive meaning: it is neither a variant nor an aberration but has specific underlying causes and recurring characteristics.

Contemporary historians of sexuality have interpreted the concept in terms of its origins in nineteenth-century medical discourse. For example, in the first volume of his *History of Sexuality*, French structuralist historian Michel Foucault identifies a number of categories of sexuality that were created in mid-nineteenth century medicine as it demarcated itself from biology. These categories, or discursive 'objects', were products of a preoccupation with four kinds of sex which Foucault describes as: the 'hyst-erization of women's bodies', the 'pedagogization of children's sex', the 'socialization of procreative behaviour', and the 'psychiatrization of perverse pleasures'. Foucault writes:

Four figures emerged from this preoccupation with sex, which mounted throughout the nineteenth century – four privileged objects of knowledge, which were also targets and anchorage points for the ventures of knowledge: the hysterical woman, the mastur-bating child, the Malthusian couple and the perverse adult.[2]

Tracing the changes that took place as medical science assumed responsibility for the production of knowledge on human sexuality, Foucault usefully suggested that concepts within a discourse must be understood as a function of power, linked ultimately to the law and the State. Understandably, such work has been very influential among contemporary social historians. It has been used to underpin much archival and political work documenting the criminalisation of homosexuality or the caricaturing of women as 'hysterical'.

One thinks of the war against masturbation that was waged within British public schools and how this related to the social production of a particular type of 'man' capable of administering the British political apparatus. In questioning the status of psychiatry as a pseudo-science, the history of sexuality implicitly offers a social determinist critique of psychoanalysis.

More recently it has been used to inaugurate Queer Theory, which celebrates the privilege of the perspectives not prescribed by the point of view that ideologies define as normal. According to Queer Theory, the word 'perversion' is nothing but an unpleasant and moralising anachronism that should be analysed in terms of its history, or else should be taken up and used ironically as an emblem of the stigma of social disapproval. Thus the contemptuous term 'pervert' becomes a badge of pride rather than a stigma, and homosexuality is simply one variant of a range of polymorphous sexualities, which differ from heterosexuality only in terms of social recognition, definition and approval.

Queer Theory also acknowledges the scapegoating of 'aberrant sexualities' which enables those 'nice normal people' to feel themselves different from (superior to) the nasty 'perverts'. Scapegoats receive projected and disowned fears of the darker side of 'normality', and are made to feel ashamed, dirty and sinful. But a celebration of 'queerness' may be (politically and personally) inadequate if it is used to deny the real predicament of a perverse subjectivity – for example, that the 'solution' created in perversion for the anxiety of sexuality is the best of all possible worlds, is superior to bland, 'normal', 'vanilla flavoured' sexuality.

Social determinism suggests that repression is a product of the censorship exercised by juridico-discursive institutions, or society, without psychological involvement. Where Queer Theory celebrates the connotations of unpleasantness, twistedness and severe moral criticism, it does so by implying that these are to be levelled at the accusers. The liberal practice associated with 'gay' politics seeks to replace the concept of perversion with the less unpleasant one of 'neo-sexualities'. Are Queer theorists and liberals right in their goal and in their strategies? What is the difference between aberrations, perversion and sexual variants?

The debates surrounding the part that the State does play, or ought to play, in prescribing, controlling and affecting sexualities continue to rage. The debates on the decriminalisation of homosexuality are well documented. Media fascination with stories of paedophilic pop stars, clergymen and social workers, bestiality, necrophilia, trans-sexuality and sado-masochism are part of an ancient, if not noble, tradition of public fascination with the grotesque.

A social determinist theory of sexuality cannot hope to account for the behaviour, actions and emotional experience of many 'perverse adults'. The events at serial killer Fred West's household in Cromwell Road, Gloucester – where home improvements and DIY were part of voyeurism, incest, sadistic torture, lesbianism, rape and murder – can only be understood if the psychoanalytic concept of the part played by unconscious sexual fantasy and 'reparative' needs in perversion is acknowledged.

On a less unpleasant level is the debate in art criticism about censorship of the portrait of child murderer Myra Hindley, made of the hand prints of children, shown at the Royal Academy of Art in the 'Sensations' exhibition of new British art. Was this a gratuitous use of the public's visceral response to the idea of child abuse which, in turn, was being abused by the artist? What is the relation between creativity and the perversions? Is there a relation between the sublime and the perverse?

A further example, which we examine more closely in this book, is the use of psychoanalysis made by film theory to understand the pleasure and fascinations of 'going to the pictures', and how the structure of fetishism is an indispensable part of following an ordinary film narrative. Here the perverse pleasures of cinema are far removed from the analysis and treatment of sadistic murder and torture, but they are nevertheless part of a psychological structure that is shared.

In the psychoanalysis of all these examples, the concept of perversion is used and the unpleasant connotations attach themselves to the actions rather than to the word itself. The word is worth some consideration, as its meaning differs considerably depending on whether it is used as a noun, adjective, adverb or verb.

As a noun it transforms a practice or person into the object of knowledge, while the subject's knowledge is the condition for freedom. Thus the nomination of an individual as a 'pervert' is a replication of the objectification and dehumanisation that is characteristic of perversion itself. Stoller, for instance, finds himself unable to use the term because of the violence and accusation it connotes. Freedom from the condition of perversion can only come from subjective consciousness.

Nomination tells us as much about the subject of science as it does about its object of study, and psychoanalysis maintains its paradoxical relation to traditional medical science by redefining the relation between object and subject. Psychoanalysis, unlike other medical sciences, suggests that there can be no knowledge of an other that is not firstly a knowledge of the self, and without this the techniques of interpreting would become meaningless intellectual games.

The verb, 'to pervert', is more colloquially associated with something that is done to the 'course of justice' and is a punishable offence, but is more commonly, in therapeutic discourses, replaced by the concept of abuse – hence 'substance abuse', 'child abuse', 'child sexual abuse', 'sexual abuse' and so on. The verb carries meanings of hydraulic metaphors of energy, bringing it alignment with divert, revert, avert and invert. (Freud's metaphors for libido, or psychic energy, took a number of forms through his work, and tended to turn towards the mechanical models of technology and engineering that had been spectacular models of progress in the last quarter of the nineteenth century.)

As a verb, it needs clarification as to what kind of activity it is, and where the energy and motivation for activity come from. A verb, like an instinct or drive, needs to have its subject, its aim and its object specified, and is less objectifying than a noun.

The adjective, 'perverse', carries less of the moralistic reproach of the noun because it is not bearing the weight of nominating the attribute of the other, it is not separating subject from object, but is qualifying the object, and when used adjectivally it may qualify a form of thinking, a structure of belief, an emotional response to life, a sexual act, an act of violence or murder. Although the adjective may be used to describe various delicious pleasures and sexual sensations that most people play around with when sexual, there is an important difference between this usage and the definition of perversion as a structure of the subject that has become a permanent and integral part of the self.

Psychoanalysis shows why this difference exists and how the latter may be positively transformed. And the purpose of psychoanalysis is to make this difference clear and meaningful. For instance, American psychoanalyst Heinz Kohut refers to this permanent and integral structure of the subject as a 'structural defect', which links this to other aspects of defensive ego development. This is further explained in the section entitled 'What Are the Post-Freudian Definitions of Perversion?' (pp. 50–62).

Freud's Early Theory of Perversion

Addressing an audience at Clark University in Worcester, Massachusetts on his first visit to what he called 'the New World', psychoanalyst Sigmund Freud presented the history of psychoanalysis, starting with the explorations into hysteria in the 1890s and tracing the developments up until the time in which he was speaking, 1909. The *Five Lectures on Psycho-Analysis*[3] gave a concise account of the dramatic revolution in understanding that had taken place over the previous decades, and presented a summary of the advances made.

Freud described his early attempts to unravel the psychological significance of bodily distress in hysteria, the effects of psychological trauma and the meaning of dreams. He concluded that:

The imperishable, repressed wishes of childhood have alone provided the power for the construction of symptoms and without them the reaction to the later traumas would have taken a different course.[4]

From the study of hysteria and dreams, Freud was then able to intuit the existence of what would become the most controversial and difficult concept of infantile sexuality. His *Three Essays on the Theory of Sexuality*[5] definitively transformed psychoanalysis from the treatment of hysteria and a new form of dream interpretation into the most significant scientific revolution of the twentieth century.

Introducing his work to his American audience, Freud acknowledged the difficulty of understanding his hypothesis, saying:

And now at last I am quite certain that I have surprised you. Is there such a thing as infantile sexuality? you will ask. Is not childhood on the contrary the period of life that is marked by the absence of the sexual instincts? No, Gentlemen, it is certainly not the case that the sexual instinct enters into children at the age of puberty in the way in which, in the gospel, the devil entered into the swine. A child has sexual instincts and activities from the first; it comes into the world with them; and after an important course of development through many stages, they lead to what is known as the normal sexuality of the adult.[6]

Freud describes the ontogenesis of human sexuality as diphasic – that is, having two waves of development: a first infantile phase, followed by a period of recession and sexual inactivity that he called latency, lasting until the hormonal and physical developments of puberty and adolescence. As the child enters the period of latency preceding adolescence, he (or she) becomes more amenable to learning from reality rather than from his own bodily experience and sexual phantasies. The infantile experiences that constitute the first of the two phases of diphasic development become repressed and form the basis of the adult unconscious mind, of phantasy and of sublimations of instincts into cultural and social practices.

By defining sexual instincts as psychological drives, expressed in an energy he called 'libido', Freud understood that sexual development in humans is not limited to genital activity in the service of the reproduction of the species, but is instinctual activity focused on a range of body organs and erotogenic zones. The principal of these are organised around the oral, anal and urethral activities of a baby's body. These are called stages of libidinal development, and refer to bodily sensations as well as ego development or cognitive development.

Although they are described as successive, the stages may overlap, occur concurrently, be interrupted and completed later. For the sake of simplicity they will be presented as if they were successive, with each phase terminating before the next begins.

The oral stage is described as the first of the stages because it is based on the neonatal suckling instinct that is observable in the foetus as well as in the newborn infant. Because the instinct serves to give pleasure as well as to ensure survival, it can be called libidinal, or sexual. The earliest libidinal activity, then, is organised around the oral organs, and its erotogenic zones are those of the mouth, lips, tongue and throat, which experience the sensual pleasures of sucking, feeding, mouthing, swallowing and later of biting and spitting.

The oral stage of development is accompanied by the development of concepts of taking in, incorporating, being merged, and during this stage the ego forms its earliest representations of the demarcation of self from not-self.

The repeated experience of the pleasurable cathexis ('charge') of libido to the erotogenic zone leaves neural memory traces that form a mental representation of an object. This mental object is a representation of the self and is also a representation of a relationship to something that was not-self. It is a component part of what will eventually become a representation of an external object, or another person. The formation of intrapsychic representations, or objects, is the basis for the ability to experience the outside world as real.

At the oral stage the outside world consists primarily of the baby's relationship with the mother, or what is sometimes called the 'need-satisfying object'. At this age the baby's dependence on the mother is absolute and so the libidinal cathexis of a pleasurable auto-erotism is linked to intense needs for survival. The experiences of excited pleasure are inseparable from experiences of life-or-death dependency. A baby's defence against this reality is partly the dependability of the maternal devotion that sustains a facilitating environment and partly a psychological one of splitting.

When the ego, or representational world, is actively using the defence of splitting, representations of pleasure are mentally separated from fears of annihil-ation or extinction. Later on, as the representational world becomes more sophisticated and better able to differentiate between different types of perception, the capacity of the ego to split off perceptions of either internal drives or external reality becomes more complex, and this defence can be found in many forms at all stages, including at the phallic phase, where it becomes a component of the perverse structure of fetishism.

Weaning With Dinosaurs

Freud's theory of instincts changed throughout his

life and therefore his understanding of sexuality also changed. We shall discuss some of the reformulations of his theory of instincts later (pp. 65–6), but for now will give a brief outline of what he considered the components of instincts and drives at the time at which he formulated his theory of perversion in the *Three Essays on the Theory of Sexuality*.

Every drive has four components: a source, a pressure, an aim and an object.

The source is somatic, an organ or group of organs from which the drive emerges. In the oral stage the source is a composite of the experiences of hunger, the sucking instinct and the erotogenic zones of the mouth. The pressure is experienced as the intensity of the demand for satisfaction that the drive exerts on the state of homeostatic stability of the psyche, or the ego.

The mental representation of the pressure of the drive is represented in phantasies of the scale of an appetite, need, craving or thirst. It can be intense, overwhelming or transient. The emergence of a drive's pressure into the psyche is usually experienced as some sort of violent intrusion of unpleasure into the pleasurable peace of rest, and this violence is often imagined as emanating from the 'outside'. Earliest defences against unpleasurable disturbances of homeostasis, or narcissistic unity, include the mechanism of projection, and this defence reinforces the ego's tendency to perceive demands on it as emanating from the outside world.

This tendency is also reinforced by the aim of a drive, which can be passive or active. The aim is fundamentally to restore the psyche to homeostatic equilibrium, and informs the ego's activities in choosing the object and action that will most successfully or immediately bring this about.

The aim relates a drive to its object. The object can be a thing, an experience, a phantasy, a person or part of a person, an action. In the case of the oral drive it might be the baby's feed from the breast, the sensation of the nipple in the mouth, the baby's ability to put his (or her) thumb in his mouth, the vocalisation of need, babbling, the exploration of a toy or new object by 'mouthing' it; it might be the desire to bite in frustration or to kiss in affection. The active aim towards the object 'a kiss' is the desire to give a kiss; the passive aim is the desire to be kissed.

The interplay of active and passive aims remains throughout drive development and takes on different meanings at different stages. British poet W. H. Auden quotes German poet Bertolt Brecht: 'The slogan of Hell: Eat or be eaten. The slogan of Heaven: Eat and be eaten.'[7]

We will return later to a further discussion of instincts and drives of what Freud calls the 'economic' aspect of sexuality, which is crucial in understanding perversion (pp. 59–62).

The ability of drives to be repressed by the ego and to be transformed into unconscious dynamics is particularly important in the course of development. As Freud said:

Even before puberty extremely energetic repressions of certain instincts have been effected under the influence of education, and mental forces such as shame, disgust and morality have been set up, which, like watchmen, maintain these repressions. So that when at puberty the high tide of sexual demands is reached, it is met by these mental reactive or resistant structures like dams, which direct its flow into what are called normal channels and make it impossible for it to reactivate the instincts that have undergone repression. It is in particular the coprophilic impulses of childhood – that is to say the desires attaching to excreta – which are submitted the most rigorously to repression, and the same is true furthermore, of fixation to the figures to which the child's original object choice was attached.[8]

That is to say, in normal development we have to give

up certain pleasurable experiences and the objects associated with them.

The anal stage then follows the oral stage. But while the former is buried, like the foundations that underlie the building of the adult ego, the experiences and phantasies of the anal stage are more actively repressed – pushed down into the basement, as it were.

As is well known, Freud saw evidence of the anal stage and its repression in the reaction formations of cleanliness, order, rigour and control. Acute embarrassment, aggressive humour or secrecy surround anal phenomena in the adult world, hinting at its continuing influence on our behaviour.

Although young children find endless amusement telling each other stories of poo poos, bums, wee wees, willies and vaginas all personified as characters in narratives of drama and action, most parents feel these stories are tiresome, boring and even embarrassing (a reaction that often adds to children's enjoyment). For adults, the protective layer of infantile amnesia means that parents do not simply revert to infancy and join in, but that the children's behaviour seems strange and irritating.

Although each phase has an aggressive aspect, where the libidinal drives become mixed with the destructive drives and become sadistic, Freud noted that aggression and sadism was particularly strong at the anal phase, which may be why such active repression is called in to master it. The positive attachments to coprophilia are linked to the pleasures of touch, texture and of smell; and sublimations of anal drives are also thought to play a significant part in much artistic creativity.

The child's ability to control the sphincter and bowel lead to feelings of power over giving and withholding, and form another set of mental representations through which the demarcation of self and not-self is built. Cultural theorists have also noted that repressed phantasies from the anal phase are much in evidence in ideologies of anti-Semitism and racism where one group preserves an idealisation of its self as 'clean' through projecting the denigrated and feared attributes of contagion, dirt and darkness to the 'other'. The forms of controlling the mechanism of separating the idealisation from the denigration usually involve physical control, such as immobilisation or ghettoisation, imprisonment and sadistic techniques of 'cleansing'. Thus the extermination camps of the Second World War Holocaust were designated the *anus mundi*.

Other kinds of narrowmindedness and cruelty have

also been linked to the anxieties and fears implicated in the anal stage.

The Excremental and the Sublime

British psychoanalyst Ernest Jones wrote:

Artistic creation serves for the expression of many emotions and ideas, love of power, sympathy at suffering, desire for ideal beauty, and so on, but – unless the term be extended to include admiration for any form whatever of perfection – it is with the last of these, beauty, that aesthetics is principally concerned; so much so that aesthetic feeling may well be defined as that which is evoked by the contemplation of beauty. Now analysis of this aspiration reveals that the chief source of its stimuli is not so much a primary impulse as a reaction, a rebellion against the coarser and more repellent aspects of material existence which psychogenetically arises from the reaction of the young child against its original excremental attachments. When we remember how extensively these repressed coprophilic tendencies contribute, in their sublimated forms, to every variety of artistic activity – to painting, sculpture and architecture on the one hand, and to music and poetry on the other – it becomes evident that in the artist's striving for beauty the fundamental part played by the primitive infantile interests is not to be ignored.[9]

These days, nursery school teachers are well aware of small children's need to play with sand, water, clay, Plasticene, play-dough and their evident delight in getting mucky. I remember as a young child going out to find the clay mud in the garden and making a head, decorated with a hairband of daisies, which I gave to my somewhat surprised mother who was washing up in the kitchen. In his essay 'The Madonna's Conception Through the Ear, A Contribution to the Relation between Aesthetics and Religion', Jones goes on to analyse the theme of Renaissance paintings of the Annunciation depicting the Angel Gabriel with lily and the Madonna receiving the word of God, and notes that:

[T]*he acts of breathing and speaking are both treated in the unconscious as equivalents of the act of passing intestinal flatus, and corresponding displacement of affect is brought about from the latter to the former ones.*[10]

Discussing the associations of blowing movement, sound, invisibility and fluidity, moisture, warmth and odour through their pictorial depiction in religious iconography and theology, Jones concludes that the Christian narrative of the immaculate conception is elaborated from an infantile sexual theory characteristic of the anal stage – that is, that babies are born out of the bottom, like faeces. These thoughts and beliefs are then repressed and become components of the adult unconscious, living on in the lives of adults as fantasy. As American psychoanalyst and psychiatrist Robert Stoller says:

Fantasy, that vehicle of hope, healer of trauma, protector from reality, concealer of truth, fixer of identity, restorer of tranquility, enemy of fear and sadness, cleanser of the soul. And creator of perversions. Since Freud first showed it we have known that in humans fantasy is as much part of the etiology of perversions – more of all sexual excitement – as are the physiological and environmental factors the sex researchers are helping us understand.[11]

The Phase of Swank and Swagger

Following the repression of the anal stage and its phantasies, the child enters a period dominated by urethral, phallic and clitoral erotism. The boy's penis, as an organ of micturition, of sensual pleasure, but especially as a visible feature, becomes especially significant; hence Freud called it the phallic phase.

This narcissistic cathexis of the penis also occurs at a time when the epistemophilic instinct is organised around the ego's use of sight, and vision is important for ego development and control. British psycho-analyst Donald Winnicott called this the phase of 'swank and swagger', because the meaning of the penis becomes attached to the aims of seeing and being seen. Here the scopophilic drive with its active, voyeuristic aim, and its passive, exhibitionistic one is integrally associated with the phallic phase. Here the distinction between female and male are discovered in relation to the visible presence or absence of the penis, so that the demarcation between self and not-self becomes symbolised by the opposition between phallic and castrated.

At the phallic phase, the male child does not associate the pleasure of the penis with the penis as organ of generation; it is a penis alone that does not acknowledge the existence of the vagina. It is at this stage that the 'nuclear complex' or Oedipus complex is at its height, and is the point at which, according to Freud, the psychological development of boys and girls becomes very different.

According to Winnicott, girls sometimes have 'a

spot of bother' at this stage, as the phallic drives are strong and girls are passionately attached to the mother as object of desire but have, as psychoanalyst Anna Freud (daughter of Sigmund) puts it, 'no executive organ of the Oedipus complex'.

In fact, both sexes meet the painful failure of their sexual pursuits, not so much by virtue of their gender, nor by the social strength of the incest taboo, but by the reality of biological insufficiency. Their organs are not organs of reproduction (are not genitals, properly speaking) and there is a real difference between the generations that cannot be ignored, denied or inverted. The difference between the generations upon which the child's Oedipus complex founders is 'castrating', as it means the child is made aware of its relative powerlessness in the human scale of things. This castration complex can take a range of representations. It is experienced as a blow to the child's narcissism or feelings of power, and represents a kind of loss that recapitulates the anxieties endured by all the preceding experiences of separation.

If the 'beneficial tragedy' (so called because it is experienced as a tragedy by the child but has a beneficial effect for society) of the castration complex is accepted and mastered by the child's ego, it leads to the primal repression of infantile sexuality and the acquisition of a more 'mature' subjectivity. The boy represses his Oedipal pursuit of his mother as sexual partner and forms an identification with his father as a model of adult destination. In doing so he internalises the failure of the Oedipus complex as a prohibition, which forms the basis for accepting the social fact of laws, rules and structures of exchange. It is at this time that the child learns social rules as well as the rules of language, dialogue, reason and the deferral of gratification (and the baffling experience of encountering this world of rules, exchange, reciprocity and taming 'wildness' is evident in boys' fascination with the game of Pokémon, and its equally baffling rules). The energies of the libidinal drives that propelled him through the developmental course of infantile sexualities are repressed and become available for sublimation through education, culture, games, sports and social activities.

The girl's journey is different as, according to Sigmund Freud, it is the castration complex that propels her into the Oedipus complex. From actively seeking the maternal object, she turns away from her mother and becomes 'daddy's little girl', actively wanting to receive from, and please, her father. This is either fully repressed and the girl, too, accepts the concept of a social law and moral code in the form of a superego, or more fluidly establishes a chain of substitute equivalents for her father's love which must be captured through seduction.

Towards the end of his life, Freud noted that his accounts of femininity were not complete, and many female analysts have proposed amendments to and developments of the Freudian theory of female sexuality. Although accounts of gender differences continue to be highly controversial topics, there is still general agreement among psychoanalysts that the pattern of an active infantile sexuality that succumbs to repression and is later revisited at puberty is a central feature of sexuality and that this diphasic nature of human sexuality is crucial to understanding neuroses and perversions.

What of the significance of the erotogenesis of other somatic functions of early childhood? The libidinal cathexis of the whole body, of the motor co-ordination of the muscular apparatus involved in crawling, learning to stand upright and walking, the fine motor control involved in writing, the acoustic and the ear as organ of reception are all significant somatic and ego experiences in early childhood. In 1938, Freud concluded that the entire body is in fact an erotogenic zone.[12]

However, of greater significance perhaps is the fact

that the development through the pre-genital stages is not only somatic but also psychological in the sense that the representations and phantasies of each stage are organised around the epistemophilic instinct and its curiosity into 'infantile sexual theories' or 'researches'. These are children's conceptual solutions to the inchoate question of where babies come from and the nature of their parents' relationship, and are 'theories' based on experience of their own auto-erotism. It is extraordinary how these intense researches of childhood, often substantiated by parents or carers, are forgotten by the time of adolescence. It is one of the contentions of psycho-analysis that these ideas and archaic solutions are still active in the unconscious mind, and indeed may form the basis of adult perversions.

Knowing and Not-knowing: The Sexual Theories of Children

These sexual 'theories' or hypotheses of children are the conceptual equivalents of the intensely physical experiences related to the erotogenic zones. Thinking is inseparable from feeling, and sensual feelings are very close to emotional feelings in childhood. In earliest childhood the merging of ego and id (instincts) creates representations in which sensory impressions are interchangeable: synaesthesia. It is the developing ego that separates sound from vision, emotional grief from physical pain, anxiety from bodily discomfort and so on, as it separates ego from id, and self from not-self. The part played by the cognate scenarios, or fantasies, of infantile sexual theories is central to this 'sorting out' of self and external reality.

We find these fantasies again in the narratives, pictures and scenarios of adult life and in culture. Although they succumb, like infantile sexuality does, to repression and to infantile amnesia, they continue to be active in the unconscious. Ernest Jones' essay on Renaissance Annunciation paintings illustrates one of the sexual theories active during the anal stage: the conception through the ear by a fart, which sounds blatantly preposterous to adult minds.[13] There are many other stories connected with laying eggs (cloacal theory), mud (Genesis) and bottoms (buggery) that gravitate around the anal phase.

The fantasies that operate around orality are also ubiquitous in culture as in children's play. Freud noted that castration anxiety might lead to a regression to an earlier stage, and describes the case of a boy who developed a fear of being eaten by his father, noting:

At this point it is impossible to forget a primitive fragment of Greek mythology which tells how Kronos the Old Father God, swallowed his children and sought to swallow his youngest son Zeus like the rest and how Zeus was saved by the craft of his mother and later on castrated his father.[14]

In a more recent version of the fantasy we can recognise in the film *Jaws* the *frisson* and thrill that derives from our identification with the killer shark and the seductive human bodies it devours. Similarly the cannibalistic murderer in the film *The Silence of the Lambs* is an ambiguous figure of appetite and of good taste. He devours his victims and also offers himself to be incorporated by the young female detective who is 'on his case'. The perverse Oedipal father in film director David Lynch's film *Blue Velvet* is associated, through the film's soundtrack and image track, with infantile greed, nursery food and an excess of bodily needs. Cinema has a particular aptitude for representing perverse or pre-genital fantasies, particularly those of orality and castration anxiety, and we shall return to explore this in more detail later (pp. 39–47).

British psychoanalyst Masud Khan's discussion of the oral phantasies that are present in perversion refers the reader to Sandor Ferenczi's theory of 'Confusion of tongues between the adult and the child' (1919), in which he describes the difference between infantile sexuality speaking a language of tenderness and adult genitality speaking a language of passion.

Fantasies from the phallic phase are easily mistaken for those of genitality because usually they refer to the (male) genital, but it is important to differentiate the infantile idea of a phallus 'alone and powerful' from the adult experience of the penis as a generative organ capable of transforming a man into a father.

Children's films and stories are a fertile source of representations of phallic fantasies, and a brief trawl is amply repaid with a rich choice of examples. Harry Potter on his Firebolt broomstick saving Griffindor (the house he was in at boarding school) by winning a game of 'quidditch' is an unambiguous story of phallic triumph.[15] The flying episodes in *Peter Pan*, *Aladdin*, *Dumbo*, *Mary Poppins*, *Bedknobs and Broomsticks*, *Chitty Chitty Bang Bang* and even *Biggles* are similar fantasies.

Although fantasies of flying may have many meanings, there is no doubt that the phallic, sexual aspect is one component of the excited pleasure in ascension. In his paper 'The Manic Defence',[16] Winnicott suggests that the idea of the 'ascensive' can be used, in the manic defence, as part of a simplified series of dyadic oppositions in which it counteracts the heavy feelings of mourning and depressive thoughts. He also suggests that the Christian representation of the crucifixion gives form to the painful affect of depressive thoughts, while the 'ascensive' movement of the Resurrection has an unmistakably phallic significance.

On Seeing as Knowing

As the phallic phase is also the time at which the scopophilic instinct is at its height, it is interesting to consider the genre of detective stories, either cinematic or literary, in this light. Boy detectives such as those in *Emil and the Detectives*, Tintin the detective reporter, Baden-Powell's boy scouts learning to identify the visual clues of nature's mysteries, boys with magnifying glasses hunting for mysteries to solve, or the private dick of the *film noir* whose voice-over monologues indicate his possession of the camera's omniscient point of view are all beautiful examples of the intense curiosity, or epistemophilia, of the phallic phase.

The fact that there is no visible object of inquiry in the Oedipal boy's quest for knowledge of the sexual other makes the scopic regime all the more frustrating, exciting and significant. Scopophilia becomes the vehicle of curiosity and the visual regime becomes sought after as the field of proof or knowledge. The phallic phase, one might say, abhors an enigma. Mystery is overlooked in favour of mastery.

What about girls' fantasies? In the phallic phase there is a capacity for penis envy, when girls wonder if they wouldn't rather be boys – or, rather, are temporarily possessed with the conviction that they would prefer to be male or have what boys have.

The Oedipal girl's sexual curiosity finds a very visible object in her father's penis, and this may remain in the adult heterosexual woman's unconscious as a feeling that men are undefinably magnificent. Penis envy subsides as the Oedipus complex arrives and girls are able to rediscover the 'loveliness' of women, of their mother, and of the idea of having a baby. The exhibitionistic side of the scopophilic instinct is often as strong as the voyeuristic, sometimes more so, and girls can become preoccupied with their appearance, with the question of whether or not they are pretty or sexy, although a girl's definition of these is rarely the same as an adult's.

Freud's theory of phallic monism led him to believe that girls and boys followed identical paths of development in the pre-Oedipal stages, and that both genders entered the phallic phase with a shared belief that all humans are endowed with a penis. It was, according to Freud, a child's discovery that girls, or women or mothers have no penis – a discovery that was effected through sight – that precipitated the castration complex and created castration anxiety.

For girls, the anxiety was a reaction to realising that they are castrated, and for boys the anxiety could oscillate between being 'about to be castrated', a threat, or being castrated, the transition towards interest in external reality.

This theory of phallic monism has been variously interpreted by subsequent analysts, and some, such as French feminist philosopher Luce Irigaray, have suggested that this is in itself an expression of a masculine 'infantile theory', which reinstates absence in the place of difference.

Of the many fantasies that gravitate around the phallic phase, some of the most interesting, from a cultural point of view, are those that find expression in the perversion fetishism. In fetishism there is a complex interrelation of a system of thought known as disavowal, based on a particular form of defensive splitting of the ego between sense perception and belief, an erotic activity or sexual practice that integrates the presence of the fetish with a particular fantasy that is essential for the experience of orgasm, and an affective structure that dictates the emotional experience of the fetishist *vis-à-vis* the fetish object and other people.

There are many psychoanalytic accounts of the analysis and treatment of fetishism, although it is widely believed that fetishism, being an imaginary solution to a universal human predicament, is rarely experienced by fetishists to be a problem.

Whereas Freud's examples of fetishistic sexual preference entailed a discussion of men who cut off women's hair ('*coupeur de nattes*'), and of the man who found certain kinds of 'shiny nose' an indispensable part of sexual excitement, we now have sex shops on the high street, bondage wear fashion as part of the mainstream and fetishism as a staple topic of late-night television. When fetishism is found in analytic treatment, the subject usually comes to be treated for some other 'presenting problem', and it is uncovered during treatment.

Apart from discussing fetishism in his *Essays on Sexuality* as a form of perversion, Freud returned to the problem in 1927 in a short paper entitled 'Fetishism'[17] and in 1938 in a posthumously published, unfinished article, 'The Splitting of the Ego in the

Processes of Defence'.[18] In the 1927 paper, Freud emphasises the part played by disavowal, showing that the choice of fetish object is usually governed by some sense perception that preceded the sight of the female genitals that invoked the terror of castration. The fetishist disavows his sense perception of the female genital and 'takes hold', to use Freud's metaphor, of some other part of the body and assigns it the role of the penis. 'It is usually something he in fact saw at the moment at which he saw the female genitals, or something that can suitably serve as substitute for the penis',[19] Freud states, and points out that the fetish indicates the subject's intention to destroy the evidence for the possibility of castration. Ironically, the fetish symbolises the genital union that it also attempts to disavow.

A Cultural Example: Fetishism and Film Spectatorship, the Theatre of Shadows

Why use a cultural example of ordinary life to illustrate 'abnormal' sexuality? It may enable us to see the universality of perverse sexuality, and to understand sexuality in its wider sense of a libidinal activity that is present in everyday life and in quite ordinary and 'normal' forms of thinking.

When we take a good look at film, infantile sexuality is neither some strange nineteenth-century scientific invention, nor is it something we need to observe in our children's behaviour. Infantile sexuality is in evidence in varied forms, sublimated in culture, or unsublimated in the behaviour of our friends, family, colleagues (criminal or not), as well as in ourselves.

The unconscious, as described by Freud, is active everywhere, and psychoanalysis, he suggested, is just a special technique for observing it in action and can sometimes even influence the course of its activity. Film spectatorship is another place for observing the activity of the mind, although it is less likely to have such an effect on it as psychoanalysis does.

We do not need to seek out 'high' art or 'grand' culture to find the grandeur of the id. Nor do we need to seek out films with overtly erotic subject matter to watch libidinal activity at work. In fact, it is much more revealing to take really popular forms like musicals, comedy, horror, sci-fi or thrillers, to find the greatest examples of the psyche in action. Horror film, the preferred cultural form of the Surrealists, has monsters from the id that are as resonant as those from Greek mythology and as meaningful as dreams remembered in the analytic setting. There are many ways in which people have applied psychoanalytic ideas to film criticism, and it is not difficult to find their books. Within this field there is a debate that centres on the use of the concept of fetishism, which is well worth exploring as it demonstrates the ubiquity of perversion in everyday life.

The concept of fetishism has been widely used in film theory to understand the compellingly pleasurable nature of spectators' identification in cinema. Christian Metz, the French structuralist who invented modern film theory, turned from semiotics to psychoanalysis, making wide use of the French psychoanalysts Octave Mannoni and Jacques Lacan. He offered an analytic theory of film in his book *The Imaginary Signifier: Psychoanalysis and Cinema*.[20] He noted that an appropriate use of psychoanalytic theory was not to be found in the 'analysis' of 'auteurs' (film directors, producers, cinematographers and so on), nor in the analysis of characters within fictions, nor even in the stories told by film (the narratives or film scripts), but that it could be aimed at understanding the mechanisms of identification that 'bind' a spectator to a spectacle; the interplay of primary and secondary identifications in the psychic apparatus and in the cinematic apparatus.

Following a description of Freud's concept of the

dreamwork, and a comparison of dream and film, Metz turns to the metapsychology to understand fetishism and disavowal, writing:

Since the famous article by Freud that inaugurated the problem, psychoanalysis has linked fetish and fetishism closely with castration and the fear it inspires. Castration, for Freud, and even more clearly for Lacan, is first of all the mother's castration, and that is why the main figures it inspires are to a certain degree common to children of both sexes. The child who sees its mother's body is constrained by way of perception – by the 'evidence of the senses' to accept that there are human beings deprived of a penis. But for a long time – and somewhere in it forever – it will not interpret this inevitable observation in terms of an anatomical difference between the sexes (= penis/ vagina). It believes that all human beings have a penis and it therefore understands what it has seen as the effect of a mutilation which redoubles its fear that it will be subjected to a similar fate (or else, in the case of the little girl after a certain age, the fear that she has already been subjected to it). Inversely, it is this very terror which is projected on to the spectacle of mother's body and invites the reading of an absence where anatomy sees a difference. The scenario of castration in its broad lines, does not differ whether one understands it, like Lacan, as an essentially symbolic drama in which castration takes over in a decisive metaphor all the losses, both real and imaginary, that the child has already suffered (birth trauma, maternal breast, excrement etc.), or whether on the contrary one tends like Freud to take that scenario slightly more literally. [21]

According to Metz (and others), the cognate structure of disavowal that consists of the oscillation between the two split off parts of the ego expresses itself, if it could be verbalised, as 'I know, but nevertheless', which is what characterises the 'acting out' in perversion. Disavowal is thus another defence that is brought into play in order to keep two split-off components of severed connection apart from one another. In perverse behaviour, a hostile drama may be enacted while the protagonist remains 'unaware' of the meaning of what he or she is doing, or 'acting out'. For example, someone being promiscuous may well assert that this is a form of sexual freedom which is nobody else's business, but also may tacitly acknowledge that the hurt or disappointment caused to others is an indispensable condition for pleasure; the role of sexual innocent who is simply being uninhibited and 'free' is an acting out of a drama of hostility and revenge.

The process of disavowal that enables suspension of disbelief is an integral part of our participation in culture generally. In reading novels the reader 'over-looks' the materiality of the text and its production in order to enter into the fiction described – just as in theatre the proscenium arch is a frame that encodes the separation of the spectators' physical reality from the space of the play that is enacted before them, and is enacted, metaphorically, within them. In both these cultural forms the materiality of the signifier – either printed words or the actors on the stage – is tangible and shared by the material presence of the spectator.

In all these forms, fetishism acts as a framing device that splits the two realities – that of sense perception and that of fictional belief – and externalises the ego's splitting.

Other forms of framing such as the play within the play (for example, Shakespeare's *Hamlet*) or the dream within the film (Hitchcock's *Spellbound*, for example) serve to reinforce the 'reality' of the framing diegesis by contrasting it with the fiction it frames.

Film differs from other dramatic arts in that it is less material and more imaginary. The experience of film spectatorship is closer to the subjective experience of dreaming or hallucination, as the boundaries between inner and outer reality become merged. This is what leads Metz to describe film as the 'imaginary signifier' and to describe the structure of representation in film as analogous to the structure of disavowal in the psychic apparatus.

When we go to the cinema we are engaged in two kinds of looking, which might be called primary and secondary identification.

Primary identification includes the pure pleasure of looking at a brightly illuminated screen while regressively nestled into darkness, warmth and a soft chair. It evokes the scopophilic instinct with its unconscious object of the mother's body and its promise of imaginary plenitude. The screen is a breast, offering itself for the gaze of an audience who have become 'Peeping Toms', sustaining excitement by the very act of looking.

Secondary identification comprises the ego's identification of parts of itself with the characters depicted within the diegesis. It embraces not only the heroes of the story, as might be expected, but the villains as well, and is effected through the way in which film narrative is conventionally constructed from a range of point-of-view shots, each assigned to the perspective of one character or another.

Secondary identifications are multiple and may be unconscious, but are represented in terms of the human form and are described as narcissistic.

Feminists, following Laura Mulvey,[22] have un-ravelled the way in which the patriarchal film form of classic realism in Hollywood cinema replicates the opposition between active/masculine/voyeuristic/sadistic and passive/feminine/exhibitionistic/maso-chistic. The narrative's progression depends on the active aim of the sadistic drive 'to make something happen', to control and to act out, and also the static, oscillating, fetishistic gaze, which halts the action and presents pure spectacle. The ratio of the two types of identification varies according to the codes of different genres; we notice it in musicals, for example, when the dramatic action is suddenly interrupted by a song and dance 'bit' and then resumes afterwards.

Mulvey is particularly accurate in showing how the cinematic representation of women in classic narrative depends on the idea of woman as signifier of castration. Woman, she notes, is either fetishised and endowed with the missing phallic attributes that make her an image of reassurance rather than anxiety (that is, beautiful rather than frightening) or is symbolically punished for bearing the lack (that is, is subjugated within the terms of the narrative), resulting in the maintenance of a fictional world in which the voyeur's need to control is shored up by the infantile 'logic' of the phallic phase.[23] The Peeping Tom looking through the window imagines that the person undressing is doing it for him and is under his magical control. Cinema makes that possible for everybody.

The fetishistic spectator is simultaneously aware of the potency of the fiction and of the technique, the filmic style, cinematography, *mise-en-scène*, lighting, use of sound, editing, intertextuality, 'for his pleasure lodges in the gap between the two'. Although this pleasure is characteristic of the cinephile, connoisseur or film critic, it is also true of people who just like 'going to the movies', because they go in order to have the experience of being carried away by the film, and also to appreciate the technique (special effects and so on) that produced this effect, and in so far as both experiences co-exist we call the film 'good' or 'well made'.

Another manifestation of fetishism in cinema is through the use of framing. Camera movement itself can be defined as a series of successive framings, and in that sense framing is fundamental to cinema, rather than a specific technique. As Metz claims:

Cinema with directly erotic subject matter deliberately plays on the edges of the frame and the progressive, if need be incomplete revelations allowed by the camera as it moves, and this is no accident. Censorship is involved here, film censorship and censorship in Freud's sense. Whether the form is static (framing) or dynamic (camera movement), the principle is the same: the point is to play simultaneously with the excitation of desire and its non-fulfilment (which is its opposite and yet creates it), by the infinite variations made possible by the studios' technique on the exact placing of the boundary that bars the look, that puts an end to, limits, the 'seen', that inaugurates the downward or upward tilt into darkness, toward the unseen, the guessed-at.[24]

Desire and its non-fulfilment is one of the essential characteristics of perversion. The pervert, one might say, is a connoisseur of desire and deferment. The metonymic movement of displacements of framing create *suspense*, which is an integral part of filmic narrative, but is also used as a specific technique in the camerawork of suspense films. The play with partial revelation and withholding, or deferment, is analogous to the metonymic structure of desire itself, and is thus sexual even when the content of these sequences is not erotic. The only difference is the pressure or *quantum* of libido that is sublimated and that which is not. Metz writes:

The way the cinema, with its wandering framings (wandering like the look and wandering like the caress), finds the means to reveal space has something to do with a kind of permanent undressing, a generalised striptease, a less direct but more perfect striptease, since it also makes it possible to dress space again, to remove from view what has previously been shown, to take back, as well as to retain (like the child at the moment of the birth of the fetish, the child who has already seen, but whose look beats a rapid retreat): a strip-tease pierced with flashbacks, inverted sequences that then give new impetus to the forward movement. [25]

What Are the Causes of Perversion?

Freud noted of the pre-genital drives and sexual theories that:

I may mention as the most important of representatives of this group the desire to cause pain (sadism) with its passive counterpart (masochism) and the active and passive desire for looking, from the former

47

of which curiosity branches off later on and from the latter the impulsion to artistic and theatrical display.[26]

The pre-genital and pre-Oedipal drives then are either repressed, sublimated or become integrated into adult genitality. If some aspect of infantile sexuality, its aims and its objects, become fixated, the drives lose their mobility, cannot move onto new objects and become stuck. The same aspect of the infantile remains active, and this may either weaken the adult sexual function acting alongside it, or even completely substitute for it. So there are ways in which some pre-genital drives may remain unintegrated into genital sexuality and may substitute their sexual aims for those of the genital zone, and this is what Freud describes as perversion:

These classes of disturbance represent direct inhibitions in the development of the sexual function; they comprise the perversions and what is by no means rare, general infantilism in sexual life.[27]

It was never clear in Freud what the cause of perversion might be. He was adamant that fixation played a part, but not sure if this was due to an excessively active erotogenic zone, infantile seduction (the sexual abuse of a child), or because of an innate constitutional 'degeneracy'.

In trying to establish the causes of perversion, Freud compared them to neuroses and concluded that while perversions and neuroses have a common origin in infantile sexuality, neuroses are the outcome of the unsuccessful repression of these drives, whereas perversions have, as it were, bypassed repression and are the result of an unsuccessful integration. Neuroses, he thought, were the 'negative' of perversions.

It is the destiny of pre-genital drives to become repressed and sublimated or to become subordinated, following puberty, to the genital drive that is directed at sexual union and intimacy with a loved person, whereupon they become component parts of the foreplay and seduction and courtship leading to sexuality proper.

Of the relation between infantile and adult sexuality, Freud suggested that:

No healthy person it appears can fail to make some addition that might be called perverse to the normal sexual aim: and the universality of this finding is in itself enough to show how inappropriate it is to use the word perversion as a term of reproach.[28]

Similarly, it may be that homosexuality and lesbianism are both an integral part of heterosexuality and differ only in the latent or overt form they take, in whether they define a sexuality or not.

What Are the Post-Freudian Definitions of Perversion?

Freud's 1938 paper entitled 'The Splitting of the Ego in the Processes of Defence'[29] proved a point of departure for other psychoanalysts. Melanie Klein took up the concept of defensive splitting and thought it originated at a much earlier stage, shortly after birth. This redefined the dating of libidinal stages, the Oedipus complex, the superego and the origins of anxiety.

Central to Klein's theory is the tenet that infancy is not only auto-erotic and narcissistic but also that it shows the existence of a complicated 'inner world' of the mind that exists from birth, which can be described as 'object relations' in the sense that the infant has internal representations of the relationships it has to significant people and things.

The central object in the infant's mind is the mother (or parts of the mother) who is both the basis of a good object, and also under constant threat of being damaged by the infant's primitive sadistic attacks.

The attack on the mother, which takes place in the phantasy life of the 'inner world', is an attack on the self and creates tremendous anxiety.

The earliest anxieties are analogous to the states of mind found in psychoses. Klein called these Paranoid/Schizoid (PS), and contrasted them to the more developed state in which an infant can recognise the effects of its aggression and mourn it, attempting to make reparation for it – Depressive position (D).

Alternation between PS and D was a perpetual feature of mental life. Splitting and projection were seen as primary defences of the PS position, while the D position allowed for creativity.

Although Klein never developed a theory of perversion as such in her work, she explored, with child analysis, the area that Freud described as children's sexual theories and was particularly interested in the early onset of sadism as an externalisation of the death instinct.

Psychoanalyst Robert Hinshelwood notes that:

Klein found that the sadistic components greatly to the fore in children, matched the kinds of sadism found in adult criminality. Subsequently Kleinians tended to regard all perversions as manifestation of the death instinct – impulses that distort sexuality.[30]

Klein's work has been both controversial and influential, and analysts working within this tradition have used her concepts to account for certain kinds of enduring negativity, as self-destructive sexualisation of the death instinct. In a moving and monumental account of his life's work with prisoners, including serial killers, murderers, rapists, child abusers and addicts, *Cruelty, Violence and Murder*,[31] Arthur Hyatt-Williams applies the Kleinian theory of the death instinct and its externalisation as aggression to the analysis of criminality, and finds in sadistic murder evidence of a perverse fantasy in which orgasm is equated with the destruction or annihilation of the idea of a baby or child. In this case there is some concept of generativity in sex, and the idea is so intolerable that it is savagely attacked in an excited and sexual way.

We can observe in most 'normal' people that the idea of their parents' sexuality is difficult to contemplate. Hyatt-Williams also notes that a traumatic experience of brutal dehumanisation is usually a part of the pathology of murder and abuse, and shows how his practice working in prisons was based on the same principles as more conventional treatments of less difficult people.

The controversy around Klein's work revolves

around her idea that infants, from birth onwards, and even before, have a complex 'inner world' which then interacts with external influences to create a human subject. Opposing this view are those such as Winnicott and others who maintain that this imputes too complex a psychological organisation too early on in infants, and that the psyche is only gradually evolved as an infant relates to its environment.

At first the baby is his mother's object and is completely dependent on her love, which constitutes his environment. Through his need to participate in this environment, the baby develops a complex representational world. This tradition gives rise to a different account of the origins and genesis of perversion, such as in the work of Masud Khan. This account represents part of a more general acknowledgement, in British culture since the Second World War, of the significance of the early dependency of infants on mothers. The work of psychoanalyst and child psychiatrist John Bowlby on attachment, separation and loss also focused on the development of subjectivity from an original dependence, using primatology as well as the study of babies and mothers. Bowlby's work developed into his Attachment theory, which establishes a very different basis for understanding the nature of infancy from that used by Klein. Bowlby did not leave a theory of perversion as such, but noted that inappropriate sexual behaviour was often manifested where attachment relations had not developed satisfactorily, or had been interrupted or severed. Perverse sexuality thus was seen as a symptom of an underlying damage to the relations of trust and security.

Perversion in this case is regarded as a distorted form of achieving contact with others. Attachment is seen as a need that is as intrinsic as any instinct, and which might well be instinctual in origin, but which makes the infant dependent on its external environment for the development of an 'inner world' or psyche.

Both Object-relations theory and Attachment theory have been very influential within psychoanalysis over the last fifty years, and analysts such as Winnicott have drawn from both traditions. For most contemporary analysts, perversions cannot be explained by the theory of the instincts alone, as regression or fixation to specific pre-genital drives and erotogenic zones or phantasies – although these certainly do play a significant part – but have to be seen as having an important dynamic aspect that relates to ego structure more widely.

For Robert Stoller, perversion is the 'erotic form of

hostility', and it is this aspect that he argues is common to all perversions. Perverse symptoms are the product of anxiety and are a response to an attack on a person's gender identity, their masculinity or femininity.

Although the acquisition of sexuality entails frustration and anxiety, this is not the same frustration and anxiety that underlies perverse symptoms. If aggression is a reaction to specific ego malfunction (either turned inwards as masochism or outwards as aggression or sadism), when this defence is cathected by the sexual instincts, particularly the regressive infantile partial drives, it becomes perverse. Thus, rape is an act of control and of violence that happens to make use of sexual organs, and not simply a sexual act that happens to be particularly aggressive.

In his detailed case studies of trans-sexuals, transvestism and pornography, Stoller traces the origins of perverse behaviour to trauma giving rise to hostility and the need for revenge. The perversion is a taking control over, and revenge against, the original trauma. Stoller also analyses the sexual component of criminal acts, even when the symptoms are not overtly erotic – describing the treatment of a woman for whom burglary became a repeated and habitual act, without erotic pleasure, although the 'breaking and entering' had the sexual meaning of intercourse in her unconscious, without her having any conscious awareness of it.

Stoller focuses on the precarious nature of masculinity as something that needs to be protected. This can be an underlying component of masculine perversions, such as a male exhibitionist who was repeatedly arrested by the police. Stoller wrote that:

Even if he is arrested he is peculiarly tranquil because the arrest indicates that he does in fact have a fine penis, powerful enough to create such a disturbance in society. We are not surprised to learn that the rate of arrest in exhibitionism is higher than any other perversion. We should not be puzzled that the exhibitionist arranges the odds so that he is more likely to be caught than any other perverse person. He aspires not to safety from the police but to safety from the inner dread of being an inadequate man.[32]

Although there have been cultures in which homosexuality was widespread, accepted and 'normative', this is not the psychological norm; and while there are tribal cultures that actively create extreme aggressivity in masculine identity, to maintain a tradition of warrior culture, and do so by creating sadistic homosexual rites of passage, Stoller argues that these are not psychologically normal. The social acceptance or prohibition of specific psychic configurations does not govern the psychological mechanism of repression and development, but merely allows this a particular manifestation or expression.

Stoller's discussion of anthropological and pseudo-scientific rationalisations for the tolerance of perverse or 'variant' sexualities is particularly telling, and points out that such work invariably elides the significance of fantasy by reducing sexuality to either biology or social behaviour.

There are many accounts of the psychoanalytic treatment of fetishism, among which the essay by Masud Khan entitled 'Fetish as Negation of the Self'[33] is illuminating and indicative of his approach to perversion more generally.

While locating fetishism within his general theory of perversion, he identifies the core characteristics of perversion by bringing together Winnicott's concept of ego development and the reparative activities of the infant towards its environment with a range of post-Freudian theories. Khan links the fetish to what Winnicott describes as 'transitional phenomena'. The transitional object is the infant's first attempt to create a symbol of a not-self; and it has meaning through the infant's subjective experience of it as animated, through its touch or smell. The object is neither destroyed nor rejected but simply loses meaning when it is no longer needed, or when attachment needs can be transformed into relationships with others. If the fetish derives some of its meaning from transitional objects, this allows us to understand a continuum of relation between pre-Oedipal and Oedipal structures, and to see the anxiety of castration as a recapitulation of earlier separation anxieties.

Khan explores perversion in terms of its function as a technique of intimacy, an alienation of self, a form of acting out and as a form of idealisation and idolisation of the self. The latter is an internalisation of the child's experience of itself as the mother's idealised 'subjective object' in the early infant-mother relationship.

Khan identifies a pathogenic relationship to the mother as the common factor in all perversions, and describes perversion as the ego's attempt at a reparative solution to the environmental failure in early ego development. He describes perverse sex as 'fucking from intent, not fucking from desire', and relates this to the perverse person's need to insert a technique of intimacy between themselves and an experience of emotional surrender.

The pervert relates not to an other in an inter-subjective encounter, but to an accomplice who is treated like a subjective object and is coerced into acting out the pervert's phantasy scenario. The need for coercion is a manifestation of the perverse person's need to control and to alienate, which leads Khan to describe the relationship of perversion as a 'contract' rather than an inter-subjectivity. It is repetitive and unchanging, and enables a specific (pre-genital) phantasy narrative to be re-enacted over and over again. Perverse people insert an object, phantasy, drama or fetish between themselves and their object of desire.

Another psychoanalyst who extends Freud's economic theory of perversion by relating it to a wider concept of ego development is Heinz Kohut. He notes that one of the interesting things that people enjoying perverse activities describe is the intensity of the pleasure they experience, which is far greater than mere genital sexuality and orgasm. He wonders why that is so.

What I am driving at is that the perversions need an explanation in which broader aspects of the total personality are considered. There are broader psychological phenomena than can possibly be defined by just looking at drive development, drive fixation and drive regression, even if we take into account the intensity of Oedipal experience and regression from it because of severe castration anxiety or ambivalence conflicts ... I do not believe that either the helplessness of the ego vis-à-vis the pre-genital addictive urge or the intense irresistible quality of the pleasure experience could possibly be an explanation of it all.[34]

Kohut specifies that he means a structured psychological syndrome rather than a playing around with pre-genital pleasures, and that such syndromes are often found as part of a series of symptoms rather than existing alone. He writes:

I have come to the conclusion that at least certain perverse symptom complexes, syndromes, can be explained . . . as sexualised versions of structural defects. In other words the structural defect (a) explains the particular weakness vis-à-vis the urge and (b) less importantly explains the intensity of the need. And it seems to me that in an addiction or a perversion the intensity of the urge is accounted for neither by the structural defect alone nor by the pre-genital fixation and regression alone, but by the convergence of both. It is the convergence of the sexual pleasure gain of the pre-genital part-instinct, added to the irresistible quality of the need to fill a structural defect, that makes the urge so intense and so irresistible.[35]

Kohut's explanation has much in common with the Winnicottian approach we find in Khan's work, in that both ascribe a reparative function to perverse action. Where Khan sees the tenderness characteristic of the infantile need, Kohut sees the weakness of the immature ego that can neither meet the demands of reality nor find the ego function to repress or sublimate the pre-genital drive that emerges from it.

Kohut's definition of a 'structural defect' is similar to Stoller's theory that trauma is an underlying component of perversion. Kohut gives the example of a man who had been unable to make a positive identification with his father, leaving him with a vulnerability in 'narcissistic equilibrium' and a need to replace intersubjectivity with a merged form of relation.

Stoller also identifies trauma as a cause of the revenge, hostility and risk that are characteristic of all perversion. For Stoller, it is especially attacks directed at the subject's gender identity, their masculinity or femininity, that are likely to give rise to perversion in adults.

Both Stoller and Kohut note that perversions are predominantly a male practice, and Stoller speculates on the vulnerability of masculine gender identification, wondering if boys are more likely to experience traumatic attacks on their masculinity in early childhood.

More recently Estella Welldon, working in London's Portman Clinic, specialising in treating perversion, has offered an account of the genesis of specifically female perversions.[36] As many psychoanalytic theories concur in identifying an infant's mothering as a cause of perversion, it is worth finding out the causes of pathogenic mothering. Welldon discusses motherhood as a role that may offer women the opportunity to act out fantasies of power, which result in infants being used as maternal objects. Welldon also analyses female perversions such as prostitution (perversion of social relations), and the possible treatment and rehabilitation of prostitutes.

Treatment

The question of the treatment and cure of perversion is difficult. It is well known that many people do not 'suffer' from perversions, but feel that, on the contrary, their actions, thoughts or feelings are what prevent them from suffering. Others have no sense at all that what they do is anything other than 'normal' or natural, or are unaware of repetitive patterns and habits of thought or action.

Because perverse practices are usually enacted within a scenario that includes what Khan calls an 'accomplice', there is the sense that they are condoned by another and therefore equal to inter-subjectivity. Some feel that their actions are permitted them by special licence, as members of a select and élite group, or that their sexuality is a superior form to ordinary and 'boring' sexuality, taking pride in their technique and specialness. This assertion of superiority may be a component of the infantile omnipotence that suffuses the pre-genital fantasies, or part of the mechanism of disavowal which implies an awareness of the inferiority of infantile sexuality to full adult heterosexual potency.

Thus very few people seek psychiatric or psycho-analytic treatment for perversions; they are felt to be the solution rather than the problem. However, many people feel shameful, that they have 'a secret', and feel endlessly dirty and sinful or afraid without knowing why.

Theory has shown that there is some psychological truth in this, as a perverse symptom may well be a defence against a dread of something more painful or dreaded, such as consciously encountering the fantasies, emotions and memories of traumas repressed and unconscious. Stoller suggests that perversion may be a defence against psychotic depression.

People seeking psychoanalysis will invariably encounter their own perversions in treatment. As infantile sexuality is, like the unconscious, universal, there is always perverse fantasy that emerges with the discovery of one's Oedipus complex and other developmental milestones. French psychoanalyst Julia Kristeva has suggested that perversion is the obverse of universality.[37] The journey is 'rich and strange', but is the best way of learning more about perversion.

Sometimes people are arrested by the police for perverse activities that are anti-social, criminal, or that have been witnessed or discovered. If so, they may receive psychiatric and psychoanalytic help in prison, remand homes or detention centres, or be referred for treatment to psychiatric hospitals; they may get help from probation officers, social workers and psychotherapists. Arthur Hyatt-Williams and Robert Stoller offer illuminating accounts of work in these contexts. There are specific questions to do with the form of treatment, the levels and timing of interpretations, the pace at which unconscious thoughts and feelings can be integrated into consciousness. Kohut suggests that too rapid a reference to sexual issues may excite a sexualised response in treatment, which masks and delays an awareness of trauma of which sexualisation can be a symptom.

In London, specialist treatment for perversions is offered by the Portman and Tavistock Clinics, which are part of the local Health Authority's provision of the National Health Service. Psychiatrists and psychoanalysts are also employed in hospitals where people may be referred for help. There is currently a greater need for help than there is adequate provision, but this is a problem of juridico-discursive and State apparatuses, and the troubled status of psychoanalysis within medical science.

Conclusion

By 1938, in 'An Outline of Psycho-Analysis',[38] Freud had considerably altered his theory of instincts. Although he considered Eros and Thanatos – the instincts of love and destruction – to be the primary forces at work in the id, he no longer considered them to be as separate as he once had.

In biological function the two basic instincts operate against each other or combine with each other. Thus the act of eating is a destruction of the object with the final aim of incorporating it, and the sexual act is an act of aggression with the purpose of the most intimate union.[39]

If sexuality and appetite are fusions of Eros and Thanatos, if seduction is an aggression, then what is love?[40]

Notes

1. R. Stoller, *Perversion: the Erotic Form of Hatred*, London: Karnac Books, 1986, p. ix.

2. M. Foucault, *History of Sexuality*, Harmondsworth: Penguin Books, 1981, p. 105.

3. S. Freud, *Five Lectures on Psycho-Analysis* (1910), in *Standard Edition of the Complete Psychological Works of Sigmund Freud* (hereafter *SE*), vol. 11, London: Hogarth Press, 1978.

4. Ibid., p. 41.

5. S. Freud, *Three Essays on the Theory of Sexuality* (1905), in *SE*, vol. 7, London: Hogarth Press, 1978, pp. 125–248.

6. S. Freud, *Five Lectures*, in *SE*, vol. 11, p. 42.

7. W. H. Auden, 'A Certain World', in *A Commonplace Book*, London: Faber and Faber, 1970, p. 134.

8. S. Freud, *Five Lectures*, in *SE*, vol. 11, p. 45.

9. E. Jones, 'The Madonna's Conception Through the Ear, A Contribution to the Relation between Aesthetics and Religion' (1914), in *Essays in Applied Psycho Analysis*, New York: Hillstone, 1974, p. 267.

10. Ibid., p. 292.

11. R. Stoller, *Perversion*, p. 55.

12. S. Freud, 'An Outline of Psycho-Analysis' (1938), in *SE*, vol. 23, London: Hogarth Press, 1978, p. 146.

13. E. Jones, 'The Madonna's Conception'.

14. S. Freud, 'An Outline of Psycho-Analysis', in *SE*, vol. 23, p. 278.

15. From *Harry Potter and the Philosopher's Stone*, the first in a successful series of children's books by J. K. Rowling, published by Bloomsbury Publishing, plc.

16. D. Winnicott, 'The Manic Defence', a paper read before the British Psycho-Analytical Society on 4 December 1935 and subsequently published in *From Paediatrics to Psycho Analysis*, London: Hogarth Press, 1987.

17. S. Freud, 'Fetishism' (1927), in *SE*, vol. 21, London: Hogarth Press, 1978, pp. 149–58.

18. S. Freud, 'The Splitting of the Ego in the Processes of Defence' (1938), in *SE*, vol. 23, London: Hogarth Press, 1978.

19. Ibid.

20. C. Metz, *The Imaginary Signifier: Psychoanalysis and Cinema*, London: Macmillan, 1982.

21. Ibid., p. 69.

22. L. Mulvey, 'Visual Pleasure and Narrative Cinema', in *Screen*, vol. 16, no. 3, London: Society for Education in Film and Television, autumn 1975, pp. 6–18.

23. Ibid.

24. C. Metz, *The Imaginary Signifier,* p. 77.

25. Ibid.

26. S. Freud, *Five Lectures*, in *SE*, vol. 11, p. 44.

27. Ibid., p. 46.

28. S. Freud, *Three Essays*, in *SE*, vol. 7, p. 191.

29. S. Freud, 'The Splitting of the Ego', in *SE*, vol. 23.

30. R. D. Hinshelwood, *A Dictionary of Kleinian Thought*, London: Free Association Books, 1991, p. 389.

31. A. Hyatt-Williams, *Cruelty, Violence and Murder*, London: Karnac Books, 1998.

32. R. Stoller, *Perversion*, p. 131.

33. M. Khan, 'Fetish as Negation of the Self', in *Alienation in Perversions*, London: Hogarth Press, 1979, pp. 139–76.

34. H. Kohut, *Lecture 1: Perversions* (7 January 1972), Chicago Institute Lectures Forum Preface, edited by Paul Tolpin and Marian Tolpin (courtesy of the Analytic Press), obtained from the Self-Psychology page at www.selfpsychology.org/

35. Ibid.

36. E. Welldon, *Mother, Madonna, Whore: The Idealisation and Denigration of Motherhood*, London: Free Association Books, 1988.

37. J. Kristeva, *Strangers to Ourselves*, New York: Columbia University Press, 1991, p. 191.

38. S. Freud, 'An Outline of Psycho-Analysis', in *SE*, vol. 23, p. 149.

39. Ibid.

40. 'The less repellent of the so-called sexual perversions are very widely diffused among the whole population, as everyone knows except medical writers upon the subject. Or, I should rather say, they know it too; only they take care to forget it at the moment when they take up their pens to write about it.' From S. Freud, 'Fragment of An Analysis of a Case of Hysteria', in *SE*, vol. 7, p. 51.

Select Bibliography

M. Foucault, *History of Sexuality*, Harmondsworth: Penguin Books, 1981.

S. Freud, *Three Essays on the Theory of Sexuality* (1905), in *Standard Edition of the Complete Psychological Works of Sigmund Freud* (hereafter *SE*), vol. 7, London: Hogarth Press, 1978.

S. Freud, *Five Lectures on Psycho-Analysis* (1910), in *SE*, vol. 11, London: Hogarth Press, 1978.

S. Freud, 'Fetishism' (1927), in *SE*, vol. 21, London: Hogarth Press, 1978.

S. Freud, 'An Outline of Psycho-Analysis' (1938), in *SE*, vol. 23, London: Hogarth Press, 1978.

S. Freud, 'The Splitting of the Ego in the Processes of Defence' (1938), in *SE*, vol. 23, London: Hogarth Press, 1978.

R. D. Hinshelwood, *A Dictionary of Kleinian Thought*, London: Free Association Books, 1991.

A. Hyatt-Williams, *Cruelty, Violence and Murder,* London: Karnac Books, 1998.

E. Jones, 'The Madonna's Conception Through the Ear, A Contribution to the Relation between Aesthetics and Religion' (1914), in *Essays in Applied Psycho Analysis*, New York: Hillstone, 1974.

M. Khan, 'Fetish as Negation of the Self', in *Alienation in Perversions*, London: Hogarth Press, 1979.

J. Kristeva, *Strangers to Ourselves*, New York: Columbia University Press, 1991.

C. Metz, *The Imaginary Signifier: Psychoanalysis and Cinema*, London: Macmillan, 1982.

R. Stoller, *Perversion: the Erotic Form of Hatred*, London: Karnac Books, 1986.

E. Welldon, *Mother, Madonna, Whore: The Idealisation and Denigration of Motherhood*, London: Free Association Books, 1988.

List of useful contacts

Portman Clinic
8 Fitzjohns Avenue
London NW3 5NA
Tel: 020 7794 8262

The Tavistock and Portman National Health
Service Trust
120 Belsize Lane
London NW3 5BA
Tel: 020 7435 7111

The Abraham A. Brill Library
http://plaza.interport.net/nypsan

The American Psychoanalytical Association
http://apsa.org/index.htm

American Psychoanalytic Foundation
http://www.cyberpsych.org/apf/

The Anna Freud Centre
http://www.annafreudcentre.org

The British Psychoanalytical Society
http://www.psychoanalysis.org.uk

Columbia Psychoanalytic Center
http://ColumbiaPsychoanalytic.org

Current Topics in Psychology: Internet Resources
http://www.tiac.net/biz/drmike/Current.shtml

Essex University Centre for Psychoanalytic Studies
http://www.essex.ac.uk/cenres/psycho

European Federation of Psychoanalytic
Psychotherapy (EFPP)
http://www.efpp.org

Free Association Books (Publisher: Psychoanalysis
& Related Topics)
http://www.fa-b.com

The Freud Museum, London
http://www.freud.org.uk

The International Association for the History of
Psychoanalysis
http://www.magic.fr/aihp/Default.htm

The International Psychoanalytical Association (IPA)
http://www.ipa.org.uk

Karnac Books (Bookseller/Publisher: Psychoanalysis
& Related Topics)
http://www.karnacbooks.com

Melanie Klein Trust
http://www.melanie-klein-trust.org.uk

The National Psychological Association for
Psychoanalysis (NPAP)
http://www.npap.org

New York Freudian Society and Institute
http://www.nyfreudian.org

Psiconet
http://www.psiconet.com

Psychoanalysis: Sources on the Internet (1)
http://www.mii.kurume-u.ac.jp/~leuers/Freud.htm

Psychoanalysis: Sources on the Internet (2)
http://www.emory.edu/INSITE/

The Psychoanalytic Connection
http://www.infohouse.com/psacnct/indbib.html

The Sigmund Freud-Museum Vienna
http://freud.t0.or.at

The Tavistock Centre
http://www.tavi-port.org

United Kingdom Council for Psychotherapy
http://www.psychotherapy.org.uk

Key Terms

Abberant: the concepts of 'abberant' and 'variant' sexualities, derived from sexology, carry connota-tions of a neutral question of difference from the norm, without such sexuality being psychologically motivated to do so. These descriptions omit (or perhaps excise) the crucial dimension of fantasy as a motivating component of sexuality.

Attachment theory: theory expounded by John Bowlby which claims that human infants, like many other primates, have instinctive and psychological needs for a relationship of dependency on a primary caretaker.

Diphasic sexuality: observation that as a species humans are unusual in having sexuality that develops in two stages: infantile libidinal development; and biological maturity.

Dyadic oppositions: a conceptual simplification imposed on the experience of complex emotional reality. The defensive use of splitting opposes two terms that separate them by replacing 'connection' with 'opposition'.

Epistemophilic instinct: the need to know and its expression in the desire to find out, or curiosity.

Genitality: the final development of human sexuality following puberty and adolescence, in which the infantile part objects become components of foreplay and the sexual pleasure of love.

Idealisation: mental process of defence in which a person is reduced to a simplified mental representation in order to defend the subject against the anxiety of ambivalence.

Infantile sexuality: theory of the onset of libidinal development organised around the non-reproductive organs of the infant's body. This is repressed with the dissolution of the Oedipus complex and exists in unconscious form, in adulthood.

Juridico-discursive institutions: concept elaborated by French structuralist Michel Foucault to describe the interrelation between ideology, politics and the law.

Libido: Sigmund Freud's concept of the mental representation of the energy of the sexual drives.

Narcissistic unity: the psychological structure that is a correlate of successful attachment relations in infancy. This continues to exist in vestigial form in the unconscious.

Object: one of the four components of a drive (source, pressure and aim being the other three). In infantile sexuality, the object is usually an aspect of a person (self or parent), a thing or a fantasy. In adult genitality, object refers to person.

Object-relations theory: Sigmund Freud's theory that all drives have an object. Developed as the most important aspect of psychology by Fairbairn, Klein and others.

Oedipus complex: Sigmund Freud's theory of the object relationship of infantile sexuality.

Ontogenesis: the process of the development of the individual, linked to the phylogenetic development of the species.

Phallic monism: theory that infantile sexuality includes a belief that all humans have a penis as the executive organ of the Oedipus complex.

Projection: a defence against psychic conflict or pain which entails a denial of awareness of an unacceptable aspect of one's own mind and the attribution of this aspect to another person or object.

Reparative need: the psychological need to repair a mental representation of a person who has been the object of attack by hostile sexual wishes. Further explanation of the reparative needs will be found in the sections, 'What Are the Causes of Perversion?' (pp. 47–50) and 'What Are the Post-Freudian Definitions of Perversion?' (pp. 50–62).

Somatic: of the soma, or body, as distinct from the psyche, or mind.

Splitting: a psychological defence entailing the severance of mental connections between two representations. If the connection creates too much anxiety or pain, splitting may bring temporary relief. This defence usually entails other defences such as projection, denial and repression.

Sublimation: the transformation of the energy of the perverse infantile drives through being directed at a different, socially useful, object. The basis of art and culture.

Variant: see Abberant.

Acknowledgements

I am very grateful to Ivan Ward, and Icon Books, for inviting me to write on perversion, and for Ivan's generosity with his extraordinary capacity for thinking. Thank you to Barry, Aldo and Theo who made time for me to work, and thank you to Rose Edgcumbe who gave me space to think.